DK eyewonder
Earth

Penguin Random House

LONDON, NEW YORK,
MELBOURNE, MUNICH, and DELHI

Written and edited by Penelope York
Designed by Cheryl Telfer and Helen Melville
Managing editor Susan Leonard
Managing art editor Cathy Chesson
Jacket design Chris Drew
Picture researcher Marie Osborn
Production Shivani Pandey
DTP designer Almudena Díaz
Consultant Chris Pellant

REVISED EDITION
DK UK
Senior editor Caroline Stamps
Senior art editor Rachael Grady
US editor Margaret Parrish
Jacket editor Manisha Majithia
Jacket designer Natasha Rees
Jacket design development manager
Sophia M. Tampakopoulos Turner
Producer (print production) Mary Slater
Producers (pre-production)
Francesca Wardell, Rachel Ng
Publisher Andrew Macintyre

DK INDIA
Senior editor Shatarupa Chaudhuri
Senior art editor Rajnish Kashyap
Editor Surbhi Nayyar Kapoor
Art editor Amit Varma
Managing editor Alka Thakur Hazarika
Managing art editor Romi Chakraborty
DTP designer Dheeraj Singh
Picture researcher Sumedha Chopra

First American Edition, 2002
This American Edition, 2015
Published in the United States by DK Publishing
4th floor, 345 Hudson Street
New York, New York 10014
13 14 15 16 17 10 9 8 7 6 5 4 3 2 1
001—196174—02/2015

A catalog record for this book is available
from the Library of Congress.
ISBN 978-1-4654-1563-9

DK books are available at special discounts when purchased in bulk
for sales promotions, premiums, fund-raising, or educational use.
For details, contact: DK Publishing Special Markets, 345 Hudson
Street, New York, New York 10014 or SpecialSales@dk.com.

Color reproduction by Scanhouse, Malaysia
Printed and bound in China by Hung Hing

Discover more at
www.dk.com

Contents

Where are we?

Where is the Earth? Good question. Let's look into space and find out where we are and what is around us. Then we'll zoom in closer.

Mercury

Venus

Earth

Mars

Sun

Let's zoom in on the Earth.

Can you see the towns?

The Earth from space
When we zoom in and take a look at our Earth from space, we can see how the countries and oceans are laid out. You are somewhere down there. This is a photograph of the US taken by a satellite.

Spotting cities
When we look a little closer, we start to see built-up city areas and green country areas. You are now looking at Florida. Can you see anyone yet?

4

The solar system

Our Earth is in the middle of a family of planets that all move around our Sun. We call this the solar system. So far, life has not been discovered on any planets other than Earth, but it soon might be one day.

Jupiter

Saturn

Uranus

Neptune

Hunting down houses

Diving down a bit, we can now see a town in Florida next door to the beach. But we still can't see any people down there.

Where are the people?

Finding people

Zoom in on a house and, at last, we can see kids! Now look back at the Earth, and you'll soon realize how big it is. It's absolutely enormous.

Crust to core

We think we know so much about the Earth and even about space, but what lies beneath our feet? Imagine that the Earth is an apple. The crust that we stand on would be as thick as the apple skin. That leaves a lot of something else underneath.

Journey to the center of the Earth

Man has only dug about 8 miles (13 km) into the Earth, which is only about a five-hundredth of the journey to the center. Scientists can only guess what is beneath, but we do know that it is very, very hot.

Earth facts

● You may think the Earth is big, but the Sun could swallow up 1,303,600 Earths.

● If you wanted to walk all the way around the Earth along the equator, then it would take you about a whole year, nonstop. You wouldn't even be able to sleep!

All around Earth is a blanket called the atmosphere, which contains the air we breathe.

The crust is the thin layer of rock that covers the Earth. It can be between 3½ and 42 miles (5 and 68 km) thick.

Granite

Basalt

Peridotite

The Earth's surface

Earth is made up of rocks. Granite is a typical continental (land) rock. Basalt is a typical ocean floor rock, and peridotite is a mantle rock.

Earth map

About 29 percent of the Earth's surface is made up of land, which is divided into seven continents (a piece of land that is not broken up by water). These are North America, South America, Europe, Africa, Australasia, Asia, and Antarctica.

People only live on 12 percent of the Earth's surface.

The mantle is the layer that lies below the crust. The deeper mantle is solid rock, but the upper layers are plastic, moving rock.

The outer core is completely liquid. It is made of iron and nickel.

The inner core is a red-hot, solid ball of molten iron and nickel that is 8,132°F (4,500°C). That's hot!

Moving world

The Earth's crust is made up of huge plates, which fit together like a jigsaw. The plates have been moving for millions of years and still shift today, with dramatic effects on the shape of our planet's surface.

The continents ride slowly on plates of crust.

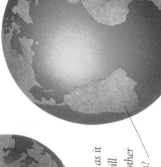

This is what the continents looked like 200 million years ago.

The continents we know today started to take shape 150 million years ago.

This is the Earth as it is today. What will it look like in another 150 million years?

Slow progress

The plates drift in certain directions. As they shift, they change in shape and size—this takes many millions of years. See what the Earth looked like 200 million years ago compared to today.

Plate line

A fault is a line along which two plates run side by side. When the plates move against each other, they can create earthquakes, volcanoes, or even mountains.

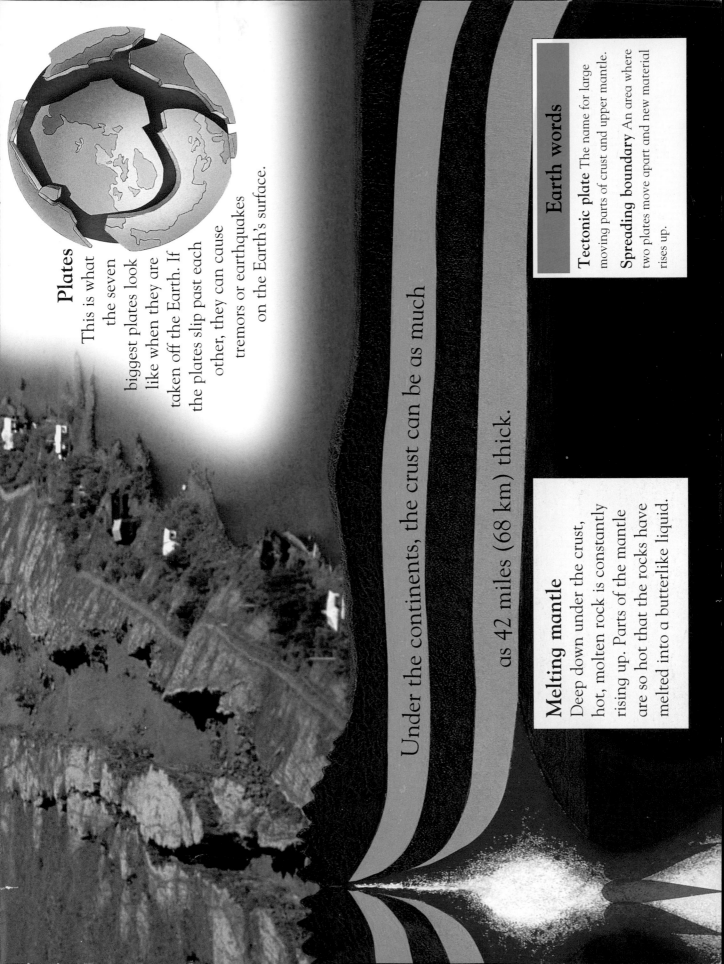

Plates

This is what the seven biggest plates look like when they are taken off the Earth. If the plates slip past each other, they can cause tremors or earthquakes on the Earth's surface.

Earth words

Tectonic plate The name for large moving parts of crust and upper mantle.

Spreading boundary An area where two plates move apart and new material rises up.

Under the continents, the crust can be as much as 42 miles (68 km) thick.

Melting mantle

Deep down under the crust, hot, molten rock is constantly rising up. Parts of the mantle are so hot that the rocks have melted into a butterlike liquid.

The tips of the world

Without mountains, the Earth would look far less spectacular. About 5 percent of the world's land surface is made up of amazing highland.

Old mountains

Mountains are made when the Earth's crust is pushed up in big folds or forced up or down in blocks. The 450 million-year-old Scottish Highlands used to be craggy like the Himalayas (below) but wind and rain have worn them down.

New mountains

The Himalayas, in Asia, are good examples of fold mountains. They are 50 million years old, which is relatively new! Mount Everest in the Himalayas is the highest point on the Earth.

The plate pushes forward slowly over the years, making more and more folds.

This model shows how plates push together, from the left side, forcing one side to crumple into mountains.

Block mountains

Block mountains are formed when the Earth's crust is moved up or down in blocks. Mount Rundle, Banff National Park, Canada, is a spectacular example of a block mountain.

Fault lines occur and a block drops or lifts to produce a high mountain and a low plain.

Hawaii is the tip of a very, very big mountain.

Underwater mountains

Long lines of islands in the oceans are actually the tips of huge mountain ranges that lie underwater. Mauna Kea, on the island of Hawaii, is the world's tallest mountain from the bottom of the sea to the tip.

The Himalayas are still rising by $^3/_{16}$ in (4 mm) every year.

The Himalayas began to form when India collided with Asia.

The fire mountain

Pressure builds up underground. Hot, liquid rock, called magma, finds its way to a weak part between the Earth's plates and explodes. Welcome to the volcano.

The big killer
The force of an exploding volcano is enormous—like opening a can of shaken soda. Chunks of molten rock as big as houses can be flung high into the air, and dust can travel as much as 13 miles (20 km) high.

Mountain makers
As the insides of the Earth explode out of the ground, the lava and ash settle, and over time a perfectly shaped mountain is formed. In effect, the Earth is turning a little bit of itself inside out.

The lava that bursts out of a volcano is 10 times hotter than boiling water.

Rivers of fire

When magma pours out of volcanoes, it is called lava. It rolls slowly downhill in a huge river, burning everything in its path. When it cools, it solidifies into rock, called igneous rock.

Bubble trouble

In some volcanic areas, you can see heat coming up from under the ground. Mud bubbles and hot water jets, called geysers, shoot up high. They sometimes smell like rotten eggs because of a gas called hydrogen sulfide.

KILLER GAS

Sometimes the gas that comes out of a volcano is poisonous. In 79 CE, Mount Vesuvius, Italy, erupted violently. A cloud of gas rolled down and poisoned many people in Pompeii, the town at its base. Ash buried them and casts have been made from the spaces the bodies left.

Earth quake!

Imagine waking up one night to find the ground trembling and shaking. That's what it's like to feel an earthquake. These sudden movements in the Earth's plates can cause terrifying damage.

Fault line

The deadly tsunami

When an earthquake happens underwater, vibrations cause ripples in the sea. They grow and grow until they are enormous, deadly waves, or tsunami, that crash onto the shore.

Whose fault?

An earthquake is caused when two of the Earth's plates slide against each other. The line that they slide along is called a fault. When they move, they cause vibrations across the ground.

Shock waves caused by an earthquake are recorded by a machine called a seismometer.

Devastation
Earthquakes can be so strong that they cause whole buildings to collapse. Children who live in areas that have earthquakes are trained regularly on how to remain safe.

The most powerful earthquakes are in Japan.

One in 1923 killed 143,000 people.

The rock cycle

Geologists divide the rocks that make up the Earth's crust into three groups: igneous, sedimentary, and metamorphic. But they all come from the same original material, which moves around in a big cycle.

You can see the different pieces of sediment in this limestone.

Igneous rock

Granite and basalt are typical examples of igneous rock. They start their lives as melted rock, such as underground magma and lava, which comes out of volcanoes.

Chalk is also a type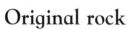

Break down

Little pieces of igneous rock are broken off by rain and wind and are carried to the sea where they pile up as layers of sediment. The remains of sea creatures are buried in the layers and may become fossils.

Original rock

Igneous rock cools down and hardens either beneath the surface or on the surface when it erupts from a volcano. It is rock from deep in the Earth's crust.

Sedimentary rock

Limestone and sandstone are typical sedimentary rocks. You can often see the layers in a big piece of rock when they have been squashed down on the seabed, such as in this photo of the Painted Desert in Arizona.

of sedimentary rock.

Metamorphic rock

Marble is a good example of this rock. It was limestone before it was changed by intense heat. When marble is polished, it produces beautiful swirly patterns.

This man is chiseling a square piece of marble from a marble quarry in Italy.

Under pressure

When sedimentary or igneous rocks are dragged deep into the Earth's crust by the moving plates, they can get hot, changing into a new rock type—metamorphic. If the rocks are taken so deep that they melt, they are back where they started as magma. The cycle starts again.

17

Vital survival

All around the Earth is a protective shield called the atmosphere. It keeps us from burning under the Sun during the day and from freezing at night. Within our atmosphere lie the water and air cycles.

The water cycle

It's incredible to imagine, but the water that we use every day is the same water that was on the Earth millions of years ago. It goes up into the clouds, and back down to the Earth as rain, and never stops its cycle.

Water goes up and

Air goes in and out

Water, water everywhere

Water goes up and water comes down. It is evaporated into the atmosphere by the Sun and turns into clouds. When the clouds cool down high up in the sky, rain falls from them.

The air cycle
The air that we breathe is also in a continuous cycle. Animals breathe in a gas called oxygen and breathe out carbon dioxide. All plants take in carbon dioxide and make oxygen.

down, up and down.

and around and around.

Essential air
Because of the air cycle between animals and plants, we could not possibly live without each other. We make the air for each other that is vital for life.

Down to earth

Without soil, life would be impossible because nothing can grow without it. Soil is the part of the Earth that lies between us and the solid bedrock.

Out of the soil grow many plants.

This level is called topsoil. It is rich in food for plants and contains living creatures.

The subsoil has less goodness for plants to feed on.

As you get lower, the soil becomes rockier.

The solid rock below the soil is called bedrock.

Useful soil

Soil can be used in so many ways, from making bricks to providing clay for pottery, but it is most vital for growing plants for us to eat. In southeast Asia, people build terraces on hillsides to stop soil from washing away when it rains.

Layers of soil

If you cut a section through the soil, down to the rock beneath, you would find lots of layers. The material nearest the top is the rich soil needed for plants to grow, and the bottom is solid rock.

A handful of soil contains about six billion bacteria!

What is soil?

Soil is made up of rocks, minerals, dead plants and animals, tiny creatures, gases, and water. As plants and animals die, tiny creatures and bacteria break them down to become soil.

Essential food
Plant roots take in nutrients and water from the soil. Plants need these in order to make food and grow.

Wriggling worms
Worms are vital to the soil. They eat decaying plants and animals and deposit them into the soil as they wriggle through it. As the worms tunnel, they help the soil to breathe.

Nature's sculptures

The moment rock is exposed to air, it is in serious danger of being reshaped. Wind, rain, air, and even plants, all seem determined to change the landscape, sometimes with beautiful results.

Frost shattering

This amazing landscape was carved by frost. Water in cracks in the rock freezes and expands and the rock shatters, leaving extraordinary, spiked shapes.

Pillars of the Earth
These strange pillars are called hoodoos. They are formed because soft rock lies below hard rock. Downpours of rain wash away the softer rock, leaving pillars of harder rock above.

Limestone sidewalk
Limestone is a soft rock that is affected dramatically by rainwater. The slightly acid rainwater changes the limestone into a softer rock, which is washed away. Cracks get larger, and the ground becomes uneven.

When air, wind, ice, or plants change the shapes of rock, it is called "weathering."

Watch out! Plant attack
Trees sometimes speed up rock cracking with their roots. As the roots grow, they creep between cracks; when they thicken, they force the cracks to open wider.

Flow of water

Water is incredibly powerful. When there is a lot of it, moving at huge speeds, it can carry away a lot of loose rock and mud. When water changes the shape of a landscape, it is called erosion.

Running wild

As water rushes from its source, in the highlands, down to the sea, it constantly picks up chunks of rock, sand, and mud along the way. It then deposits these elsewhere, changing the shape of the land as it goes.

This harder rock is left behind after floods.

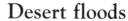

Desert floods

Water can even shape the desert. Heavy floods sometimes rush through the land, taking the soil with it and leaving weird towers of rock behind, such as in Monument Valley, Arizona.

Water power

The Grand Canyon is the largest gorge in the world. It has been carved by the Colorado River over 20 million years. Different rocks react in different ways to the water, so the shapes are incredibly spectacular.

Niagara Falls

Niagara Falls is an
enormous waterfall that
moves backward by 3 ft 3 in (1 m)
each year. The lower rock is soft
and is worn away by the water.
Eventually, the top rock crashes
to the bottom when it can
no longer stay where it
is without support.

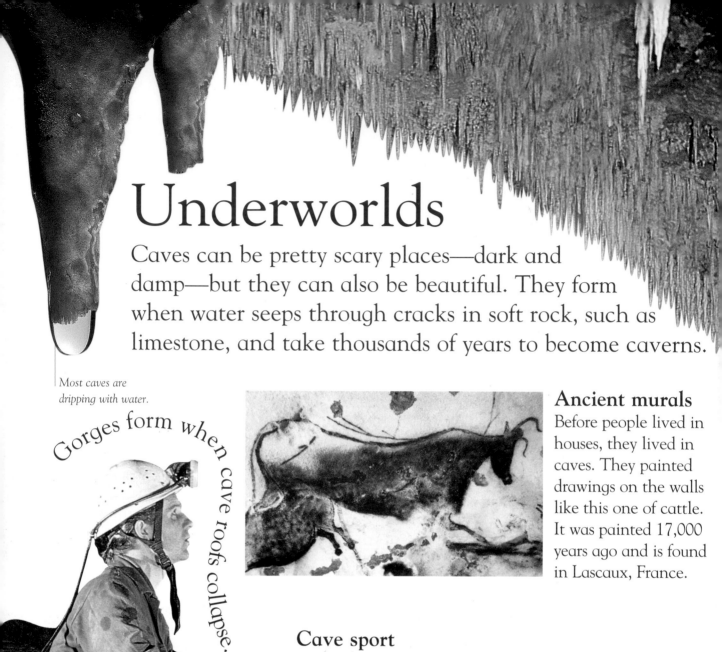

Underworlds

Caves can be pretty scary places—dark and damp—but they can also be beautiful. They form when water seeps through cracks in soft rock, such as limestone, and take thousands of years to become caverns.

Most caves are dripping with water.

Gorges form when cave roofs collapse.

Ancient murals

Before people lived in houses, they lived in caves. They painted drawings on the walls like this one of cattle. It was painted 17,000 years ago and is found in Lascaux, France.

Cave sport

Caves may be dark, but they are also magical, underground landscapes, and some people enjoy exploring them as a hobby. This is known as spelunking. It's a very dangerous sport, however, and must always be done using the right equipment.

The biggest cave in the world, the Son Doong Cave, Vietnam, could fit hundreds of tennis courts inside it.

It can take thousands of years for stalactites and stalagmites to meet.

Up and down
When water drips from a cave's ceiling, it leaves behind tiny pieces of rock. Over many years, the pieces grow downward into a long icicle shape called a stalactite. Where the water falls to the ground, stalagmites grow upward like candles.

The power of ice

There's more to snow and ice than meets the eye. Not only do they produce some of the most spectacular scenes on the Earth, but they are also powerful tools that sculpt it.

Earth's natural plow

A glacier is an enormous mass of ice that flows downhill slowly. When glaciers melt, they show how much of the soil has been carried away. You can see how a glacier has shaped this Norwegian fjord.

The mighty glacier

A glacier is incredibly powerful. It carves its way through mountains, leaving huge gorges or valleys behind. On the way it swallows up and moves giant boulders. Yet it only moves at a speed of about an inch a day.

Floating island

Some icebergs are huge. But whatever you see above water, there is even more below. Two-thirds lies underwater.

Ice caves

Icebergs are big blocks of ice that break away from the end of a glacier. As they melt, the wind and waves batter them into weird shapes, sometimes creating ice caves.

The mighty wave

When you play on a sandy beach, have you ever noticed how often the waves crash onto it? Well, believe it or not, that wave movement is constantly changing the coastline. Waves are even powerful enough to reshape cliffs!

Waves destroy

Shock waves

● As the waves force coastlines back, sometimes houses built on the cliffs fall into the sea!

● A series of pounding 33-ft- (10-m-) high storm waves can remove more than 3 ft (1 m) of cliff in one night.

Making a bay

The sea is very persistent. When it finds a weak part along a coast, it breaks through and spreads out as far as it can. It eventually creates a bay, such as Wineglass Bay in Tasmania.

some coasts but make brand-new beaches elsewhere.

Creating sand

Sandy beaches take hundreds of years to form. Waves near the shore pummel boulders into pebbles, and with more battering they eventually become the soft, fine-grained sand that you find on a beach.

It's amazing that water alone can turn this pebble into fine sand.

Coastline sculpture

This picture shows how powerful waves are. The sea has completely battered its way through the rock on this cliff and formed an archway. Eventually, when the arch gets too weak, it falls in on itself, leaving stacks behind.

The ocean floor

The ocean is a mysterious place—we can't go beyond certain depths because the pressure will kill us. We do know, however, that the ocean floor has some features that are very similar to those found on land.

Earth oceans

More than two-thirds of the Earth is covered in water. The deepest part of the ocean is the Mariana Trench in the Pacific Ocean; it is 7 miles (11.5 km) deep. Very little life can survive in those depths.

Black smokers

Where the ocean plates move against each other, vents open and hot steam rises into the water. These are called black smokers.

Coral from surface to ⅓ mile (0.5 km)

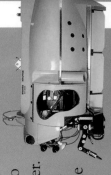

Coral reef

Coral reefs are found in clear, warm waters near the shore. Corals are living things and are home to hundreds of others as well.

Diving down

It is very difficult for humans or submarines to go down deep underwater. This submarine is called the Nautile and can take three people down to depths of 2½ miles (4 km).

Submarine 2½ miles (4 km)

Hatchet fish 6 miles (10 km)

Ocean floor 7 miles (11.5 km)

Pillow lava
Where volcanoes erupt on the ocean floor, the lava solidifies into round, pillow shapes in the water.

Hatchet fish
The hatchet fish is one of the few creatures that can survive in the deepest parts of the ocean.

There are many massive abysses on the ocean floor.

Exploding ground
Volcanoes and earthquakes happen underwater, where the plates meet, just like they do on the land's surface.

Earth's treasures

Hidden deep underground lies a priceless treasure trove of precious minerals, which includes rocks, metals, and crystals. We are constantly digging into the Earth to find these minerals because we use them all the time.

Jewel in the crown

Most gems that you find on valuable jewelry start their lives in rock. They begin as crystals but, after they are cut and polished, they end up as beautiful and expensive gems.

Gold diggers

To find precious metals and gems, we have to mine for them, and sometimes they are hard to get at. Tons of rock, for example, may only hold a few ounces of gold.

Gold and silver have been used to make coins and jewelry for thousands of years.

A dash of salt

I bet you wouldn't eat jewelry. Well, gems are crystals and so is the salt that you sprinkle on your food. Pools of seawater are left to evaporate, leaving the salt behind ready to be collected (right).

Mineral facts

● Diamonds are one of the hardest substances. They are used in drill bits, or to cut glass.

● Talcum powder is actually a mineral called talc. It is very soft and crumbles easily.

● Silicon, which is obtained from minerals such as quartz, is essential in the making of computers and cell phones.

Earth's ingredients

Inside the Earth's crust are some essential ingredients called fossil fuels—coal, gas, and oil. We use these to provide energy that runs everything from cars to the electricity in our homes.

Treasure from the Earth

Believe it or not, the coal we burn in our fires used to be trees that lived between 280 and 345 million years ago. Their remains didn't rot fully and over time became coal.

Mining for coal

When coal was first discovered, it was quarried from the surface. Today, there are many deep mines, as well as huge surface mines.

Treasure from the sea

Oil and gas were tiny sea creatures that died millions of years ago and were buried under the seafloor. Eventually they became oil. Often, gas is found just above the oil.

Sometimes oil is piped straight to the mainland, but often huge ships called oil tankers take the oil away from the rigs.

Oil rigs

A lot of oil and gas are found in rocks below the seabed, so the only way to get them is to drill deep below the ocean. Oil rigs are platforms in the ocean that are specially built so that we can drill for oil and gas from them.

Oil facts

● Oil is used for many things, such as gas for trains and planes, and power plants. Even the ink on this page is made from oil.

● Workers live on oil rigs for weeks at a time. Their supplies are flown in by helicopter.

Sea creatures

Rock

We use fossil fuels all over our homes. Some stoves use gas.

Gas

Oil

Rock creatures

Fossils are the remains of plants or animals that have been preserved in rocks over millions of years.

Fossil facts

● Fossils show that starfish lived more than 450 million years ago.

● Dinosaurs appeared about 240 million years ago.

● The oldest fossil is 3 billion years old and is a microscopic bloblike creature.

Ground detectives

We know a lot about the Earth's history because, amazingly, the Earth tells us all about it. Fossils and layers of rock found deep underground help us to understand the mysteries of the past.

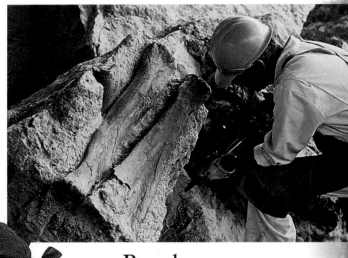

Rock strata

Each layer, or stratum, in this cliff in Utah tells a different story. The top layers are 10 million years old, and the gray areas near the bottom are about 210 million years old. Dinosaur footprints have been found in this layer.

Trapped in time

Amber is fossilized tree resin or gum. Millions of years ago, insects were trapped in amber and remain to this day. Because of this, we have proof that spiders have existed for a long time.

Bare bones

We know that dinosaurs roamed the Earth millions of years ago because we have found many of their bones fossilized into rocks.

By putting all the bones together it is possible to see what shape the dinosaurs were.

Different worlds

The Earth has so many different climates, weather systems, and types of rock that no one place is the same as another. Animals and plants have had to adapt to each place so they are also very different. Take a look at some of the worlds within our world.

The rain forest

Plants can easily grow in areas that have huge amounts of rainfall, such as some places in South America. The rain forest has so much rain that the area is covered in plants. There are lots of animals here because there is so much food to eat.

The desert

Deserts are the driest places on Earth. They are often in regions that get little rain, such as Africa. Not much can live there.

The city

Over thousands of years, people have taken over large areas of the Earth and built huge towns and cities on them. A lot of settlements are built near water because it is essential for our survival.

Coldest areas

The top and bottom of the world—the Poles—are the coldest places on Earth, and only a few animals can live there. Penguins thrive in the freezing conditions of Antarctica.

Planet pollution

The Earth is a special but fragile place. Some of the things we do to it, such as polluting it with chemicals, are destroying resources that are valuable to its survival. We must learn to look after our home.

Growing deserts

Deserts are constantly expanding. People living near them use up plants for food or fuel, and once land becomes a desert it is difficult for anything to grow there again.

Burning forests

Since 1945, more than 40 percent of the world's tropical rain forest has been cut down for lumber and farming. When forests disappear, so do many animal and plant homes.

A lot of garbage

Think about how much garbage you throw away in your home. Now imagine everyone else's garbage added to it. It's a big problem.

Polluted air

Factories, especially those that run on fossil fuels, pump dangerous chemicals into the air that are bad for our lungs. They also make the rain acidic.

A big waste

Each day, a huge amount of sewage and chemical waste from factories is pumped into our rivers and oceans. Dirty water can spread diseases and can kill fish and other wildlife.

OIL CRISIS

On March 24, 1989, the giant oil tanker *Exxon Valdez* had an accident in Alaska. Within a few days, it spilt 11 million gallons (42 million liters) of oil into the sea. The oil polluted the shoreline and killed huge numbers of fish and birds. It took years to clean up.

Planet protection

How can we protect our planet? Conservation means trying to maintain the planet and not destroy habitats by dumping waste. When the situation gets bad, here are ways that we can help.

The wind makes the turbines spin around really fast, which creates energy.

Garbage cleanup
To solve the garbage problem, we need to recycle more of our trash. Bottles, paper, plastics, and all kinds of other materials can be used again and not buried in the ground.

Wind power
Burning fossil fuels to make electricity puts poisonous gases into the air. Fossil fuels can be replaced with wind turbines. These wind farms are clean and safe for the Earth.

Only about 400 of these beautiful Siberian tigers still live in the wild.

Endangered species
There are many animals, such as this tiger, that have lost their homes. Others have been hunted to extinction. Zoos now breed animals and release them back into the wild.

A tree nursery

An excellent way to save the rain forests and to stop deserts from growing is to replant trees as we chop them down. We will always need wood, but if we plant new seeds, like these children in India are doing, we will never run out of trees.

Protection facts

● Car exhausts throw bad chemicals into the air. In the future, our cars may run on power from sunlight, called solar power.

● To help keep rivers and oceans clean, make sure you never drop any litter into them.

Which way?

Help the submarine reach the coast from the depths of the ocean. Answer the questions correctly to find the way up!

Seawolf

Mount McKinley

Vinson Massif

Which is the world's tallest underwater mountain?
See page 11

geyser

blowhole

Hot steam rising from ocean floor vents is called a...
See page 32

black smoker

Mariana Trench

Tonga Trench

The deepest part of the Pacific Ocean is the...
See page 32

START

FINISH

The submarine that can take three people down to a depth of 2½ miles (4 km) is…
See page 32

Nautile

where water is warm

where plates meet

Mauna Kea

Argonaut

forms metamorphic rocks

Volcanoes and earthquakes happen underwater…
See page 33

solidifies into pillow shapes

floats around

where abysses exist

Where volcanoes erupt on the ocean floor, the lava…
See page 33

Romanch Trench

True or false?

The Earth is full of amazing things. Do you think these statements are true or false? You can find the answers in the book.

Gold has never been used to make coins.
See page 34

Penguins thrive in the freezing conditions of Antarctica.
See page 41

The solid rock immediately below the soil is called crust.
See page 20

Granite is fossilized tree resin or gum.
See page 39

Hatchet fish can survive in the deepest parts of the ocean.
See page 33

Submarines are used for exploring deep underwater.
See page 32

The Earth is divided into seven continents.
See page 7

Animals breathe in carbon dioxide and breathe out oxygen.
See page 19

Dinosaurs appeared about 20 million years ago.
See page 38

Basalt is a typical ocean floor rock.
See page 6

When air, wind, ice, or plants change the shapes of rock, it is called "weathering."
See page 23

World tour

Grab your passport and tour Earth's amazing features in this race. Who will be the first to fill their passport with stamps and make it to the finish line?

Catch a plane to Europe. **Move forward 4**

Take a flight over Niagara Falls. **Move forward 2**

Take a detour around the Grand Canyon. **Go back 6**

Surf across to the US. **Move forward 3**

Avoid an erupting volcano. **Go back 5**

Cruise over the ocean. **Move forward 4**

How to play

This game is for up to four players.

 Move down   **Move up**

You will need
A die
Counters—one for each player
Trace over the footprint outlines or cut and color your own from cardboard. Each player takes turns throwing the die and begins from the START box. Follow the squares with each roll of the die. If you land on an instruction, make sure you do as it says. Good luck!

START

Wait for summer
to warm up
Siberia.
Skip a turn

FINISH
**Good job! You're the
winning Earth explorer!**

Go hiking
in the Alps.
Go back 3

Find a shortcut
through caves.
Move forward 2

Stop to mine for
precious stones.
Skip a turn

Lost in the
Australian
rain forest.
Skip a turn

Blown back by
an Antarctic
storm.
Go back 2

Strike oil!
**Throw
again**

What's this?

Take a look at these close-ups of pictures in the book and see if you can identify them. The clues should help you!

♣ They cover about 5% of the world's land surface.

♣ They are made when the Earth's crust is pushed up in big folds or blocks.

See page 10

♣ It pours out of volcanoes.

♣ It is 10 times hotter than boiling water in a kettle.

♣ On cooling, it solidifies.

See page 13

♣ Limestone is a good example of this type of rock.

♣ This type of rock has layers.

See page 17

♣ These can be formed by an underwater earthquake.

♣ They can build up to become deadly waves.

See page 14

♣ This thin layer of rock covers the Earth's surface.

♣ It can be between 3½ and 42 miles (5 and 68 km) thick.

See page 6

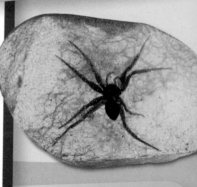

- These are the driest places on Earth.
- They are often found in regions that get little rain, such as Africa.

See page 40

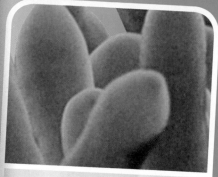

- These are found in clear, warm waters.
- They are living things and are home to other creatures as well.

See page 32

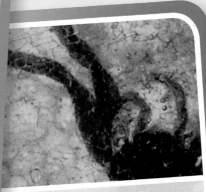

- This is fossilized tree resin or gum.
- Millions of years ago, insects got trapped in it.

See page 39

- They look similar to long icicles.
- They are formed when water drips from a cave's ceiling.

See page 27

- These big blocks of ice break away from glaciers.
- Two-thirds of this block of ice lies underwater.

See page 29

- They are strangely shaped pillars.
- They form when rain washes away soft rock, exposing hard rock.

See page 23

Glossary

Here are the meanings of some of the words that are useful to know when learning about the Earth.

Atmosphere the blanket around the Earth that holds in gases.

Bacteria miniature living things, invisible to the eye, that help to convert dead plants and animals back into soil matter.

Carbon dioxide an invisible gas in the air that animals breathe out.

Climate the average weather in a particular area.

Coastline the place where land and ocean meet.

Conservation to keep things the same and undamaged.

Continent one of seven huge areas of land on the Earth that are not broken up by sea.

Coral reef a mass of rocklike material that is formed by skeletons on the ocean floor near to the ocean's surface.

Core the hot, central part of the Earth.

Crust the hard outer coating of the Earth that is made from solid rock.

Desert a very dry place that has less than 10 in (25 cm) of rain a year, which is very little.

Earthquake sudden movements in the Earth's crust that cause the ground to shake violently.

Equator the imaginary circle that passes around the center of the Earth, between the poles.

Erosion when rock or soil is loosened and transported by glaciers, rivers, wind, and waves.

Fault a break in rocks with plates moving on each side.

Fossil remains of living things that have been preserved in rocks.

Fossil fuel fuels that include natural gas, oil, or coal, all of which are natural and are formed by dead prehistoric animals or plants.

Glacier mass of ice and snow flowing slowly downhill under its own weight.

Gorge a deep narrow valley cut by a river.

Igneous rock a rock that starts as magma below the surface of the Earth but hardens either underground or on the surface.

Lava red, hot, melted rock that pours out of a volcano when it erupts and then solidifies.

Limestone a sedimentary rock composed mainly of calcium carbonate.

Magma rock that has melted to a butterlike fluid beneath the Earth's surface.

Mantle the part of the Earth immediately beneath the crust.

Metamorphic rock a rock that has been changed by underground heat or weight.

Mineral a simple substance that, either alone or mixed with other minerals, makes up rocks.

Ocean a huge, salty body of water; also called a sea.

Oxygen an invisible gas in the air that animals breathe in order to survive.

Planet a large, round object that orbits a star such as our Sun.

Plate a separate section of the Earth's crust that rides on the semiliquid rock of the mantle.

Pollution materials and gases that are in the wrong place and spoil that environment for the plants and creatures that live there.

Rain forest a tropical forest that receives heavy rainfall and therefore where huge amounts of plants grow.

Rock a large, solid mass underground that is sometimes exposed at the surface of the Earth and is made up of one or more minerals.

Satellite an object in space that revolves around the Earth.

Sedimentary rock a rock formed in layers by the deposition of eroded grains.

Seismometer an instrument that measures the strength of earthquakes.

Sewage garbage or waste that is carried away in sewers.

Solar power energy that is gained by using the Sun.

Solar system our family of eight planets that revolve around our Sun.

Stack a rock pillar left standing in coastal waters when the top of an arch collapses.

Stalactite a hanging, icicle-shaped structure formed in caves by dripping water with traces of rock in it.

Stalagmite a rising candle-shaped structure formed when stalactites drip to the floor and leave traces of rock behind.

Strata layers of sedimentary rock.

Tsunami a huge, fast-traveling wave that is caused by an underground earthquake.

Volcano where hot magma breaks through the Earth's crust with great pressure.

Weathering the breaking up of rocks by wind, rain, or ice.

Index

Acknowledgments

Dorling Kindersley would like to thank:
Dorian Spencer Davies for original illustrations; Jonathan Brooks for picture library services.

Picture credits:

The publisher would like to thank the following for their kind permission to reproduce their photographs:
a=above; c=center; b=below; l=left; r=right; t=top

Ardea London Ltd: Graham Robertson 39l. **Bruce Coleman Ltd:** 19t, 40tr, 40br, 44bl; Jules Cowan 22; Pacific Stock 32-3. **Corbis:** 14-5, 21, 23tl, 28-9b, 28-9t, 28r, 29tl, 29r, 32c, 54, 55, 56 boarder; Archivo Iconograofico 26c; Hubert Sadler 16l; Stuart Westmorland 4-5b; Ted Spiegel 17r; Tom Bean 16-7, 52cl, 53br, Hal Beral 53tc, Ralph A. Clevenger 53c, Albert Lleal / Minden Pictures 51cl. **Dorling Kindersley:** Dreamstime: Clearviewstock 4-5 (background), Pearson Education Ltd 51br, Peter Griffiths - modelmaker 48bl, Rough Guides 52tr, 52c, 53tl, Coleman Yuen / Pearson Education Asia Ltd 50br. **Dreamstime.com:** Alexyndr 48tr, Anetlanda 48crb, Shariff Che'Lah 51cra, Doughnuts64 49br, Jan Martin Will / Freezingpictures 48c. **Environmental Images:** Herbert Giradet 42tl. **Gables:**27r. GeoScience Features. **Fotolia:** Pekka Jaakkola / Luminis 50tc, Zee 50bc. **Getty Images:** joSon / Iconica 19br, Telegraph Colour Library 52bc. **Picture Library:** 39cr. **Robert Harding Picture Library:** 10tr, 16cl; Thomas Laird 10c. **Hutchison Library:** 40main. **The Image Bank/Getty Images:** 1, 4cr, 24c, 37r. **Masterfile UK:** 23br, 36c, 40l, 56c; John Foster 24l. **N.A.S.A.:** 4-5t, 7t. **Natural History Museum:** 17tr. **N.H.P.A.:** Anthony Bannister 34tl; Haroldo Palo Jr. & Alberto Nardi 26-7; Robert Thomas 26bl. **NHPA / Photoshot:** Haroldo Palo Jr 53cl. **Photolibrary:** Radius Images 50cl; **Planetary Visions:** 2, 18-9, 40tc, 40cr, 40bl, 41tc. **Powerstock Photolibrary:** 3, 18b. **Rafn Hafnfjord:** 8-9. **Science Photo Library:** 4-5ca, 12-3, 20l; B. Murton 32-3b, 33tl; Bernhard Edmaier 12l; David Nunuk 23tr, 53bl; ESA 4cl; G. Brad Lewis 13t; Martin Bond 25, 30. **Still Pictures:** 34c, 34-5, 36bl, 41r, 42cr, 42b, 43, 44cl, 45. **Corbis Stock Market:** 24bc. **Stone/Getty Images:** 11tl, 14l, 19b, 30-1, 31t. **Telegraph Colour Library/Getty Images:** 5br, 14c, 20c.

All other images: © Dorling Kindersley.
For further information see **www.dkimages.com**